MW00776198

Me, Myself & Allah

Me, Myself
&
Allah

Elham Rammouni

2023

First, I want to thank Allah for all aspects of my life, the joys and the challenges, the highs and the lows.

I now understand that everything I experienced, even the hardships and the hurting, were all an expression of his love; Allah does not test us to forsake us; he tests us only to bring us back to him, our ultimate savior.

dedication

To Allah, my eternal guide,

In the pages of "Me, Myself, and Allah,"
I dedicate this humble endeavor,
In pursuit of healing and self-discovery,
With faith as my compass, and your light as
my tether.

With love and devotion,
Elham Rammouni

Contents

Bis-mi-lah

بسم الله

With God's blessings

على بركة الله

Chapter one

Me & Myself:
Battles within

I can see her in school next to a window
It's a sunny day
It's only 10 AM
A fragile heart

A busy mind
Wondering, dreaming, and planning
Two years from now
Five years from now
And even dare to think ten years from now
How she'll make it to college
How she'll act, learn, live, and love in life
She knew the world was scary
But nothing was as she had seen
Soon to hit her 30s
Now she's alone in her room
It's a rainy day
It's 2 AM
A broken heart
A mad mind
Reminiscing, overthinking, and praying
It's sad to see now, how
Little did that girl know.

Darkroom

falling tears,
I have scars all over me,
broken pieces, all that I see,
no solution in sight,
neither far or near,
yet I whisper a prayer in between.

Me, Myself & Allah

I dream of unattainable greatness,
And the bitter soul knows
It knows its destiny,
The world won't set it free
Toward the light is its only path,
Everything is holding a grip on my heart
Unable to reach my feelings,
Nothing is helping, not the raindrops,
Not the wild waves,
Not the slow melody,
Unsure of how it's supposed to be,
I have been pulling away all along,
It'll feel unreal to go back,
Been looking at the star for far too long,
It'll feel unreal to reach and grab it,
You can't always get what you want in life,
we are meant to catch and let go,
You can hold on so tight,
You can hold for so long,
But eventually, you'll let go,
Nothing has to do with you,
It's just the way it goes,
And sometimes it's the way it's supposed to go,
If you can fathom that,
Then maybe life will hurt a little less.

Ya Rab, give me the strength to keep going.

You'd think the winter's breeze is cold.

It's nothing
compared
to these
midnight
thoughts.

The girl who seemed unbreakable, broke.

She dropped the fake smile
and whispered,
 " I can't do this anymore ..."

Ya Allah, Ya Kareem*,
be her guiding light in the shadows,
grant her solace,
and empower her to rebuild herself once
more.

*Kareem= The Most Generous

Now my clock is my enemy,
Every second it's passing, it's mocking me,
It's whispering answers I don't want to hear
Tick tock, tick tock.
No, he's not. No, he's not
The echo in my ear,

Tick tock, tick tock.
You. Are. Not. Enough.
Tick tock, tick tock.
You will do what I want,
Tick tock, tick tock.
Your thoughts are mine now,
Tick tock, tick tock.
You. Are. Not. Enough.
Tick tock, tick tock, tick tock.
When. Will. This. All. Stop.
Ya Rab! Ya, Raheem*!

*Raheem= The Bestower of Mercy

To my past self,

Sorry I couldn't be there as much as I should have.

Those who saw pain,

can loudly read   those who suffer
in silence.

Me, Myself & Allah

I'm lying in bed, in my house,
and all I want to do is go home.
When home is not a place,
The heart will forever be on a chase.

You try so hard to relate,
and you try so hard to connect,
but you've been detached.
Not a soul,
not a memory,
not a dream,
then I recall,

        Allah is always near,
his infinite mercy and love are greater than
anything.

In a world spinning out of control,
Who am I to stay sane?
The line between evil and good is thinner
than ever.

Their faces, life, and words,
they're all bogus.
I have no interest in the superficial world we
live in.
Is the true meaning of life still out there?
Or has it been ruined just like their minds?

Ya Rab, Ya Lateef*,
give us patience, peace, and reconnect us
with the truth.

*Lateef= The Most Gentle

I wish I was fighting an open war,
but it's just one war after another with me.

I just want peace,
but I feel that I won't get it anytime soon,
not till everything has been wrecked.

You don't know real pain,
till you place your hand on your heart,
tears rolling down,

reciting Quran to help mend the shattered
pieces within.

I pray that on our saddest, loneliest and
weakest moments,
Allah SWT guides us to raise our hands
and make Dua.

And through his words, we start to heal.

Chapter two

Me,
Myself,
& Allah:

A journey of Faith
and Healing.

It took me many challenging years,
but I found Allah SWT eventually.

I'm now content and at peace.
And my heart is filled with gratitude.

-Alhamdulillah (Praise be to Allah)

Pray that you'll be strong
to the point you're not in life,
but with Allah SWT,
even when you're weak,
you're still the strongest you'll ever be.
Shed tears; Allah SWT listens attentively.
So, make Duas, and rest assured,
he will respond.

Prayers with tears,
the most powerful therapy you'll receive.

- And it's absolutely *for free!*

Every night,
I turn to Allah,
praying for peace and protection.
Leaving my worries and heartache
to Allah's care.

- tawakal

In Makkah,
I was alive again.

In Madina, I was in love again.

Islam does not reject sadness,
nor prevent tears;
but how you handle these emotions,
demonstrate your true faith in Allah

I'm sorry if you're feeling weak again.
I'm sorry these thoughts are in your mind
again; please put all these thoughts into
your prayers.

Raise your hands and let it out.
Cry, pray, then pray again.

Ya Rab! Ya Mujeeb*

*Mujeeb=The Answerer

You should know you're only a human,
and you'll never be able to see the whole
picture;
maybe you will and perhaps you won't,
but Allah SWT can.

In a way your brain can never comprehend.
Rather than searching for reasons, have
complete trust and deep faith that it's all
ultimately in your best interests.

Tell a tired heart, there's Sujood.

And tell a broken heart, there's qiyam.

I have left many broken pieces on that praying mat.

-   The correct method to heal.

I know you want something from Allah SWT,
but how many times have you prayed for it?
How many times have you called his name
and asked Allah for it?

- **Be *relentless in your Dua***

Allah SWT healed me,

When no one else saw my wound.
for his mercy reaches beyond what human
eyes can perceive.

When everyone else chose to judge me,

Allah SWT granted me pardon.

Allah SWT loved me when nobody else did

Every day,
I try to live in accordance
with the principles of Islam,
and sometimes I fail;

Ya Allah, ya Haleem*

I beseech you to lead me closer to you,
let your blessings fill the gaps where I fall
short.

*Haleem= The Most Forbearing

Read about our Prophets;
read about our Islam;

it'll enlighten your mind,
and soften your heart.

In times of doubt, turn to the Quran

And seek guidance through prayer.

I may feel weak at times,
but that's alright.
I've learned how to find strength within
myself, through my connection with
Allah, Al-Qawiyy*.

*Al-Qawiyy= The all Strong

Life is constantly changing,
So I constantly pray for myself.

I pray for my heart,
I pray for my mind,
And I pray for my soul,

to stay on the **righteous path.**

Do we constantly need a reminder from the less fortunate to know how blessed we are?.

We have much more than we think,
We all do.

Always say Al-Hamdulillah and be content with what Allah gave you, and he will bless you even more.

Some of Our Prophet's PBUH last words
were:
Salat, salat, salat*!
Maintain your salat.

So, prioritize your salat over any social
media obsession.

* Salat= Prayer

Our Salat is a shield that blocks
immoral sins, fear, and wicked deeds.

It protects us from negativity and opens the
doors to numerous blessings.

Life can be overwhelming at times;
it's okay to escape from it all,
but seek refuge in Allah SWT, Al-Qadir*

not in any of this Dunya's destructive,
useless and
temporary pleasures.

*Al-Qadir= The Capable

Wake up,

read your
Morning Azkar,
pray,
Tawakal,

then start your day.

I encourage you to continually learn about
Islam,
and read about the life of Prophet
Muhammad PBUH,

not merely for memorization,
but to embody its teachings to your daily life.

Let it shape your character.

Something about being in our
Prophet's PBUH
favorite city that just rejuvenates me.

I miss being in Madina.

Today's quote of the day

"Keep your sorrows at bay

by reciting a Surah each day."

I asked Allah SWT for courage and success.

As I live my life
I embrace the path ahead
and remain mindful
of the opportunities
that he will present in my path,
to change for
what he knows to be best for my life.

Do I think that life is cruel and unfair?
Yes, but then I remember there is Jannah

Our relationship

with Allah SWT

should be firmer and stronger,

than any other relationship we have in this world.

Key to happiness:

Build a strong and consistent relationship
with **Allah** SWT.

Chapter three

Close to Allah:
A Blessed Journey

So distant from today's world,

but so close to
Allah SWT.

- *best companionship*

Keep working on your deen.

Keep working on it,
till you're blessed to see our beloved Prophet
Muhammad PBUH,
in your dream.

I prayed to Allah SWT for Al-Ferdaws
- the highest level of Jannah-

And I will trust the path,

Allah will put me through to get there.

Sinners;
I don't judge you,
one day I was you.
So I solely pray for you,

I pray you rediscover the path to Allah SWT,
as his forgiveness awaits you when you
sincerely repent and seek his mercy.

May your journey with Allah SWT

always be a round trip.

Islam is not complicated; humans are.

Allah SWT does not rebel nor resent a sinner;

Allah SWT, Al-Ghafoor*,
he forgives and pardons.

Al-Ghafoor= The Forgiving

On my bucket list:

I pray that I am blessed to see our beloved Prophet Mohammad PBUH in my dream.

\-   About me:

I don't trust a Godless heart

Life is tough,
and it demands daily faith renewal.
Though you might face moments of
weakness,
do your best to find even the tiniest bit of
strength to avoid sinful people, situations,
and places.

Keep Allah in mind always,
stay committed to being a good Muslim.

I pray for you,
I pray that no matter what road you go
through,

your last destination leads you to Allah SWT.

Surely, you must know.
You know,

What's preventing your prayers from being
answered?

Not every day is a good day;
live anyway.
Not everyone will like your way;
keep going anyway.
Even when the world is too blind to see,
and not many will believe,
it's enough that **Allah** SWT knows.
With a heart as pure and strong as yours,
never let it fade away.
Keep your eyes wide open at your dreams,
never let it gaze away.
Your road is a tough one to take,
It won't always shine,
Just don't lose your faith,
And it all will turn out fine.

Every new morning

is a chance
to be closer to Allah.

A chance
to repent,

and a chance
to become a better muslim.

In the dark
I like to sleep,

but in my grave,
Allah's light,
I hope to see.

Ya Allah, As-Samad*,
I ask you for a good end.

*As-Samad= The Eternal, Self- sufficient

I pray you and I
live a righteous life just as our Prophet
Muhammad PBUH did.

I pray you and I
find virtuous companions like those our
Prophet Muhammad PBUH had.

I pray you and I
experience the love and mercy our beloved
Prophet Muhammad PBUH displayed with his
spouses.

Live a righteous life before it's your moment of truth.

- - **your grave**

This Dunya is not meant for you.

Don't be misguided,
and let it consume you.

We are Allah's creation, destined to return.

and what we do for him is all that will last,
our true concern.

<u>Reminder</u>

Don't risk
Jannah
for
this
Dunya.

Hold on firmly
to the rope of
Allah SWT,
never letting go,
no matter how tough it gets.

Trust in him,
and he will guide you through.
Stay firm in your faith.

Chapter four

Sin's Shadow:
Seeking Forgiveness and Mercy

Sad fact:

Our generation is the closest one to another,

but sadly the farthest one from Allah SWT.

Me, Myself & Allah

Watching the world around me,
a moment of silence consumes me.

It pains me to see,
the religion that once moved seas,
now is consumed by social media screens.

Out of place I feel,
don't any of them think,
How will our Prophet feel?
Our generation needs to heal.

Ya Rab, Ya Mateen*,
please keep our heart firm on your deen and
on your straight path.

*Mateen= The Steadfast

Actions speak louder than words when it comes to one's deen.
So, don't trust those who speak highly of their deen,

until you have witnessed their actions.

Sad Truth in today's world

Mainstream culture > Deen

Haram relationships > Halal relationships

Wickedness > Righteousness

Ya **Allah**, Ya Jabbar*

so many broken and lost young hearts in our
time;
fill them with your love, guidance and mercy.

*Jabbar= The Restorer

Doesn't it scare you that you daily live in sin,
and assume you're winning in life?

Eventually, your sins will catch up to you and
take you down.

Ask yourself if your current lifestyle is
suitable for your hereafter?

And remember Allah's doors of forgiveness
are always open, Al-Tawwab*,

and his mercy is boundless.

*Al-Tawwab= The Ever-Pardoning

Moment of realization;
the sins that led to the destruction of the
previous Prophets' towns and their people.

These same sins still exist within our society
today.

Ya Allah, Ya Hafiz*,
Shield us from these sins,
and keep us steadfast on your religion.

*Hafiz=The all protecting

This generation,
with its social media obsession,

it's blinding and disturbing.

FYI,
just because you are famous in this Dunya
does not make you famous in the heavens.

Social media itself is not a weapon;
it's your actions that wield its impact.
Take charge of how you utilize it and decide
its effectiveness.

Be cautious of who you follow,
what you allow yourself to absorb,
and what takes up your time.
To make the most of it, filter your social
media feed and opt for content that nurtures
your soul, purifies your heart, and enlightens
your mind.

I fear for the future of our children and their descendants;

Ya Allah, Ya Haadi*

I earnestly beseech you to guide them towards embracing your true Islamic religion, and the teachings of our Prophet Muhammad PBUH.

Steering them away from the mainstream practices prevalent among many modern muslims.

May their devotion to the true essence of Islam deepen, leading to a meaningful and fulfilling righteous path.

*Haadi= The Guide

Raise your kids to memorize the Quran;
it'll be their immunity from today's society.

Ya Allah, Ya Wadood*,
bless our children with comprehension and
understanding of the Quran, lead them to its
teachings, and keep them away from
anything that contradicts it.

*Wadood= The Most Loving

Practice Islam sincerely with your heart,
for if it doesn't truly resonate within,
all efforts are in vain.

On judgment day,
if your heart lacks belief,
your tongue will expose you.

It's not enough that you're born muslim;
if Islam doesn't reside in your heart,
strive to find it.

And pray for the opportunity to strengthen
your faith and commitment to the deen.

If learning about Islam does not make you a
better person,
then,

relearn it.

Patience is the correct answer to any of life's hardships and dilemmas.

It is the ultimate test.

Faith is more than just knowing theoretical concepts;

It becomes meaningful when it is accompanied by actions that show our belief and faith.

So, demonstrate your love for Allah SWT

by dedicating more time in worship, actively engage in Islamic learning,

and help others through sadaqah and zakat.

Here's a prayer
for you and me,
on the difficult days;

Ya Allah, Ya Rahman*,
lead us to the straight path.

And bestow upon us
the wisdom
and determination
to overcome
the challenges of this temporary life.

May your blessings and mercy be upon us
always.

*Rahman= The Most Merciful

In the depths of the night,

the best opportunity
for Tawbah.

Ya Allah, Al-'Afuww*

Please accept our repentance,
and forgive all our sins,
the ones that we are aware of,
and those that are hidden from everyone.

*Al-'Afuww= The Pardoner and forgiving

Chapter five

The Journey Beyond: Embracing Infinity

We should never
forget,
that
our life on
this earth is
only a fraction
of our true journey,
and death is not the final destination.

It's the end of the beginning,
-judgment day-

The beginning of eternal bliss and peace
or eternal torment.

Heaven or Hell.

Death
is not a reminder to live your life;
it's a reminder
to know why you're in this life,

to worship Allah SWT.
Al-Baaqi*

*Al-Baaqi= The Everlasting

The purpose of life for each of us,
is to strive to live in accordance with the
commandments of Allah SWT and the
teachings of Prophet Muhammad PBUH.

Aspiring to be the best possible Muslims.

This involves living in virtue, kindness, and
righteousness, constantly seeking
improvement in our faith and actions.

It is through this path that we find fulfillment
and achieve our highest potential as
individuals and as part of the Muslim
community

Do not live your life
in hatred and injustice.

The wrongdoers will suffer the most from
Allah's wrath.

Allah grants respite but does not neglect.
Keep that in mind.

As believers,
we should place our utmost reliance and
unwavering trust in the hands

of Allah SWT, Al-Nafi'*,

Knowing that only he can help, heal, guide,
and give provisions and blessings.

We must understand that his mercy and
grace encompass all aspects of our life, and
nothing can occur until he decrees it.

*Al-Nafi'= The benefactor

Ya Allah, Ya Azeez*

Please bless me with inner peace,

and the unwavering commitment

to faithfully worship you,

and abide by your commands.

*Azeez= The All Mighty

Self-awareness is crucial in understanding
our relationship with Allah SWT.
Regularly reflect on your actions, words and
thoughts to better understand how they align
with your faith and make improvements.

Strive to lead a life filled with good deeds,
repentance, and I'badat*.

*I'badat= Worship

It is crucial to always keep in mind,
that death
is the universal truth,
an inevitable fate for everyone,
and it does not discriminate.

Thus, we should live each day with sincerity
for the hereafter.

Turning to Allah

especially
during hardships

showcases true faith.

Remember Allah consistently
in your daily life,
not only in times of need.

Ya Allah, bring us closer to you,
the closeness of a beloved servant not only a
needy servant.

We should
remain steadfast
in our trust in Allah SWT,
as we earnestly seek
his mercy,
hoping for the best in life to come.

Ya Allah, Ya Hameed*,

Help us remember and appreciate the
blessings you have bestowed upon us,

and always remain
thankful and grateful to You.

*Hameed= The Praiseworthy

As Muslims,

we should stay humble,
kind-hearted,
committed to Islam,

and true to our faith.

Ya Allah, Al-Wakil*,

Grant us the strength and resilience to practice our Islamic beliefs daily,

and to stay committed no matter the challenges we encounter each day.

*Al-Wakil= The Trustee

Ya Allah,
grant me
a trustful,
content,
honest,
and
a sound heart.

To navigate through life
easily and truthfully.

In life,
let's constantly remind each other of our
fundamental duties:

Worship Allah, be mindful of our words,
refrain from committing sins and injustice,
and do good deeds.

Because hereafter is what truly matters,
with **Jannah** as our ultimate goal.

Let's conclude it with the remembrance of
Allah SWT

SubhanAllah
سبحان الله

Al-Hamdullah
الحمد لله

La Ilaha IllaAllah
لا إله إلا الله

Muhammad Rasul Allah PBUH
محمد رسول الله

Allahu Akbar
الله أكبر

Astaghfirullah
أستغفر الله

Despite the prevailing injustice, immorality, and corruption in the world, there is still goodness and righteousness that exists in our world.

Among the global community, there remains a minority of Muslims who strive to uphold and spread the true Islamic teachings and beliefs.

Aspire to be part of this righteous group, and even if you find yourself distant from it at the moment, remember that Allah, the greatest, surpasses any sin, and his mercy embraces all.

Let us all draw inspiration from these devoted muslims and strive to make a positive difference in our own lives and communities.

Pop quiz:

Out of Allah's 99 names, how many were used in this book?

Hope you've been counting =)

Me, Myself & Allah

Made in the USA
Monee, IL
24 July 2023

39781875R00066